HIGH FLYER

flying far above the rest

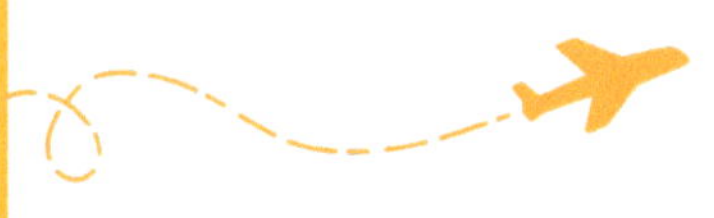

By Ashton Bohannon

DEDICATION PAGE

For my son Gianni, who has always had a love of
aircraft. May the Lord elevate you to heights
beyond your imagination.

If you are willing and obedient,
you will eat the good things of the land;

ISAIAH 1:19

You hear that the sky is the limit,
but is this really true?
No, of course not! God's plan
expands further than you knew.

God wants to take you higher—
high up in the sky.
He wants you to live a life beyond
the human eye.

You're going outside of the limits and beyond the bounds that people place on other human beings because God wants you to live as part of outer space.

God made the heavens, and He made the earth too.

He wants you to live your life like you are aware of this truth.

The big blue sky that is vast and wide.
There's so much to learn, so you must ask why.

Why did God make all of this—the moon, the stars, the sun, and the sea?
He made it for us to enjoy, yes; He made it for you and for me.

*God designed everything
according to His plan.
He breathed His special life power
into His man.*

*God will show you secrets of the
world if you are His friend.
He shows you how to expand,
expand, expand.*

*God never wanted people to live a regular life.
He wanted us to continuously learn how to take flight.*

*We are supposed to fly higher and become so much more.
God plans to give us more than we could even dream or wish for.*

God will guide us on our journey through the timeless heavenly space, but we must stay close to Him as His friend and keep Him in the right place.

God must be first and never last. And if we keep this promise, He will put us in first class.

First class is a place where rich
people can sit,
And we can only sit there if we hear
God's truth and obey it.

God wants to get His message to all
the ends of the earth.
But He can only do this when we
agree to work.

*We must listen to Him and work, using our faith.
It is the only way we won't crash or be late.*

*There is a route, a way we should go.
We can get there in any conditions,
whether rain, sleet, or snow.*

*No matter the weather, the season, or the place,
God is unlimited, and He will let us go at an accelerated rate.*

*Because God maps out the route and gives us a plan.
He shows us the way outside of the way of man.*

For God to guide us, the onditions don't have to be just right.
He can do it at any time, whether it is day or it is night.

That is the amazing thing about God.
He can do anything against any odds.

God works with us and gives us insight.
He shows us what's true and what is right.

God makes us soar, going straight through the sky—
the same sky that keeps most people inside.

Locked inside the world and
unable to see, simply because
they can't believe.

But zoom, zoom! All who believe
zoom through the sky.
After we get the power and
choose to ignore the devil's lies.

It is possible to work with God
as His ambassadors,
and because of Him, we move
ever faster.

Faster, faster, yes, faster than
the rest.
It is because we are one with
God that we are the best.

*Separately called and set apart.
Different than the others because we
have been given a new heart.*

*A heart, a mind, a way to think
God keeps us operating on a full
tank.*

We are connected to the Creator of the world.
He owns it all—never forget the gates to His house are pearls!

So yes, of course we occupy a place.
A place that is far beyond the common space.

There is a spirit realm, and it is real.
It transcends and extends way
beyond everything we see and feel.

Feelings, thoughts, they can tell lies.
We must not trust them ecause it
isn't us on whom we rely.

*We can pass, and we can fly.
We can go way beyond the sky.*

God is a Spirit—a Spirit we can see, taste, and feel—supernatural because this xperience exists outside of what most think is real.

They see life as normal and very mundane.
That isn't for us. We aren't the same.

There are so many things we can't see with our human eyes,
but when you trust God, He shows you how to navigate these skies.

He is a leader, like a man who can drive.
With God, we will be safe as we go for our ride.

Our ride up to heaven, where we can sit
next to Jesus Christ, the co-maker of it.

Jesus Christ, the Son of the Father,
is how
we can become more, right stinkin' now.

He took our sin, and He made us new.
He did something only God could do.

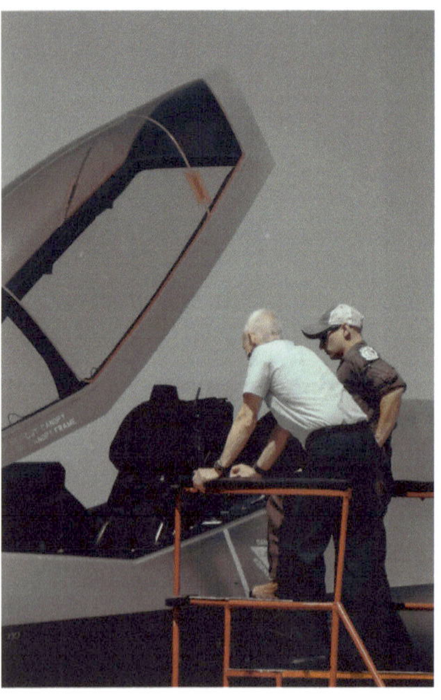

We didn't deserve the tickets to sit here.
But thank heaven that Jesus has brought us near!

Near to the Father by removing our sin so our mistakes are forgiven, never remembered again.

All you must do if you want
to fly high and know
what all is out there is simply
to go!

Go to the Father through
Jesus Christ.
He sits beside Him. This isn't
a heist!

We don't have to steal or trick or slide.
God gives us a way to spiritually hide.

Hide from our enemies and become brand new.
He gives us a way to be guided on what else to do.

After you change and go to a new place,
You will be different even if you have the
same old face.

It isn't external, the change that you see.
It happens inside you, setting you free.

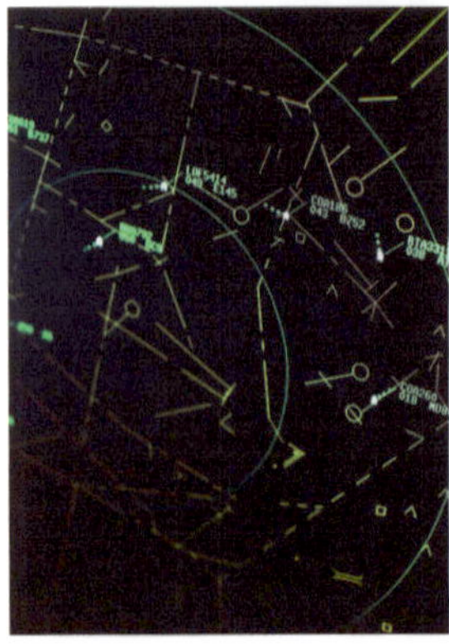

God gives you a guide, an inside navigator.
A system that leads you, a spirit trafficator.

God is the air traffic control man sitting in space.
He knows what will happen and He sees your fate.

Sunset

He sends you His Spirit, the Holy Ghost.
Now you are moving and able to coast.

Coast across distances you never could go
without the help of the Spirit, that is fo' sho'.

*As you trust His commands and you go the right way,
There is no limit, just yourself, that could make you stay.*

*Stay at a lower level and stay down below.
That isn't my place, and now I know.*

I know I am an aircraft created for
so much more.
I don't live life like it is a chore.

This isn't a game to be taken lightly.
I must stay focused and do it rightly.

*Not with my own effort—no, of course not.
I would mess it up if I were simply trying a lot.*

*I am not trying. I don't have to strive.
I just focus on God, and He helps me to glide.*

With God, I can glide right through the air.
Man, this is awesome, and I'm not even halfway there.

How much higher can I go?
It's wild, a surprise, like I'm watching a show.

God's incredible power is a surprising wonder.
What else in the world will God help me to plunder?

Trust in God, and trust in His plan, and know when you're saved, you're no longer a mortal man.

You will succeed, and it will be great.
With God, you become heaven's first mate.

Wait, what? Are we on a boat?
Ha-ha, look up—not even close!

*Just when you think you have seen all you can see,
God will show you that this is only the bottom of the trees.*

*Look up and look beyond.
You just started! This is only a pond.*

There is so much you don't yet perceive.
Oh, my goodness. The plane has yet to
leave!

I thought this whole time I was already in
the sky.
"Tee-hee," says God, "now enjoy the ride."

If you fully obey the LORD your God and carefully follow all his commands I give you today, the LORD your God will set you high above all the nations on earth.

Deuteronomy 28:1